MW01290484

SWEDISH DEATH CLEANING

FOR BEGINNERS

How to Declutter and Downsize your way to

a happy home and life

By

Sarah Hodges

Copy right © Sarah Hodges

All rights reserved.

This book is a property of the author and shall not be reproduced or distributed without express consent.

ISBN: 9781729290361

TABLE OF CONTENT

Preface

Death might be such a cold word but it is the inevitable fate of every human. It is not absurd to prepare for your death by putting certain measures in place before that time comes. Making the most out of the life we have now is what creates the perfect memories to look back at even when this phase is over.

After a person's demise, the family and friends are often plunged into a painful phase of grief which is grouped into five stages namely; denial, anger, depression, bargaining and finally acceptance. At some point, they have to deal with putting away the personal effects of the deceased which is never easy.

The art of Swedish death cleaning is aimed at curtailing the trauma of losing someone. What's a better legacy to leave behind than to ease the bereavement process of those we love?

While compiling this book, it came to mind that this subject may be strange to a lot of readers, sometimes we death-clean without even knowing it is a concept on its own with many amazing benefits.

Decongesting space and living in a clutter-free environment doesn't only provide health benefits, it also plays a significant role in psychological wellbeing. The title of this book may have struck your thoughts leaving you with questions like "what is death cleaning?" "Why death clean?" "Is it for just Swedish folks?"

This book will provide all of the answers you need while helping you learn how to stay clutter free.

CHAPTER ONE

Swedish Death Cleaning

Sweden is a Scandinavian nation famous for many things such as IKEA, ABBA, meatballs, and of course, 'The Gentle Art of Swedish Death Cleaning'.

To put it simply, the art of Swedish death cleaning is about ridding your home of possessions that you don't want, need or use, so when you do happen to kick the bucket, your loved ones are not left with the grave emotional task of sifting through 80+ years of your stuff. It's a blatantly honest approach to decluttering your home and a very transparent way to look at all the things that you possess.

"Döstädning" which means "Death Cleaning" in English, is a new method of downsizing and organizing. The art of Swedish death cleaning cannot be discussed without mentioning the Swedish author and artist Margareta Magnusson.

The approach is designed as an easy way for folks over fifty years of age to purge their homes and organize their possessions in hopes that their children won't be overburdened by their belongings once they pass away. Although this sounds morbid, it is actually a pretty smart idea.

Death cleaning is not about getting rid of all your stuff, but rather streamlining your life so you're only holding onto what makes you happy. Death cleaning is not just about dusting or mopping up, it is about a permanent form of organization that makes your everyday life run more smoothly.

The background

This new cleaning phenomenon is not about dusting, vacuuming and other traditional cleaning practices, rather about a holistic approach to a 'clutter-free-and-care-free' home. On a lighter note, I'm sure you have looked at a pile of dusty books, stared at an old pile of magazines or pushed aside a pile of well-worn clothes and thought, I really should just get rid of all this stuff.

The concept

The concept of actually cleaning out your house in preparation for your imminent death is called Döstädning. Dö means death in Swedish dialect and städning means cleaning. It is the process of organizing earthly possessions before death so that the emotional burden is alleviated for the family and loved ones. The Swedes start the process of 'dostadning' as early as 50. Little by little, people try to sort out each room of their homes by removing possessions they simply don't need, want or use anymore. It is an exacting cull that requires the individual to rip off the proverbially band aid and say goodbye to all the stuff taking up too much space in the home and the mind.

The process of dostadning takes the pressure off a huge clean-up later in life therefore allowing people take their time to really declutter and sort out their things; the process is a continual one. One motto to live by is "if you don't love it, lose it. If you don't use it, lose it". This is easier said than done, especially if you have a tendency to hoard your possessions or struggle to part with them because of sentimental value or other reasons. The rule of thumb is to keep only what you love and what truly makes you happy in the moment.

Why you should give Swedish death cleaning a try

It is possible to get rid of anything and everything. If you don't love it, don't use it, or don't need it, you can get rid of it. This would include books, clothes, knick-knacks, and just about anything else. Your apartment, house, room, or homestead is your big cluttered oyster, ready to be-clutter free thanks to this philosophy.

The art of Swedish death cleaning is not about recklessly throwing your possessions out without a second thought. The second step is making conscious decisions about where your old things would be kept or put away. A popular idiom states that one man's trash is another man's treasure. Instead of giving your friend a new bunch of flowers to show appreciation to them, you could give them some of your books you no longer need. Improvise.

Try selling some things on eBay, donating to homes Or if you're no longer loving that tea set you thought you wanted when you first moved into your house because you wanted to seem sophisticated, you could give it to your aunt as a present next time she visits. It isn't about shifting where the clutter stays, but gifting it to the appropriate people.

The art of a good death clean is about throwing away things that you no longer love and keeping the things that you need all for your greater benefit. Life is made up of good and bad memories so why keep sectors of those memories that aren't necessarily happy ones? Learn to pass on memories, whether it's in the form of books, clothes, cards etc to those around you for new memories to be made with the lucky new owner of your things.

The process of undertaking Swedish death cleaning isn't meant to trigger thoughts about your transience but rather ignite a new found sense of peace from your clutter-free home. A house full of possessions can trigger anxiety, so by adopting the principles of Swedish death cleaning, you are actually enhancing your wellbeing. In essence, the philosophy has more to do with a better life. After all, we are living longer, accumulating more stuff and hanging on to things that we just need to let go.

Start small e.g. one room at a time and declutter what you can. Take small steps over a longer period of time, rather than one big clean out over a frantic weekend. See how you feel after one room has been decluttered and also how you feel knowing your possessions are now prized possessions to someone else.

Chapter Two

Decluttering

To Declutter means to remove unnecessary items from an untidy or overcrowded place. Although the word is defined this way, decluttering your home doesn't necessarily mean that your house is untidy or a stockpile of items. It simply involves sorting out the stuff you do not need or haven't used in a long time. It is said that if you haven't made use of an item for over a year then you can probably do without it.

When you start going through all your stuff, you may find that you tend to get sentimental about certain items. Even with items you never liked or used, you make mental excuses and come up with possible future uses. You might even come up with emotional associations and reasons why parting with an item is not the best decision (for example, "I can't give out this scarf, my first ex-boyfriend's mum made it for me"). If you listen to what's going on in your head, you would realize that it is not always logical. Here's one way to declutter your space without being overly sentimental.

The Six-Month Clutter Rule

This requires you to make a commitment of getting rid of anything you have not used in the past six months. Generally speaking, if you haven't used something in six months, you're almost surely never going to use it although there are some salient exceptions e.g.

- Seasonal items - These are items used during different several seasons of the year e.g. holiday decorations like Easter eggs, Hanukkah candles or Christmas trees.

- Special clothing for occasions – You may have a special outfit selected to be worn on certain occasions. You could store this away until it's no longer what you would wear on that occasion.

- Items you didn't get a chance to use - If you bought an item and did not get to use it during that span of time, give it another six months. If you still haven't used it by then, consider whether you're really ever going to "get around to it" someday.

- Gifts from kids - Kids are the exception to every rule. Just because you don't use that funny-looking painted tray your kid made in art class doesn't mean you should part with it.

- Mementos - With souvenirs and mementos, you may not use them every six months. Instead, consider how strong your emotional attachment is to them. If it's not doing much for you anymore, then there's no reason to keep it.

One of the biggest challenges is the rationalization that you are bound to encounter. It is even more difficult because these rationalizations will come from within. If you are to effectively carry out a thorough death clean, you must first learn to push through these rationalizations.

1. It could come in handy - Sure it could, but for someone else. If you haven't used it in the last six months, maybe that someone isn't you.

2. It cost a lot - It's painful to get rid of stuff you once paid dearly for. It may mean you wasted money or got taken in by a gimmick. But keeping the item isn't going to turn a bad purchase into a good one.

Don't let your mistakes own you. Learn from it and move on. Besides, a valuable item could be turned into cash on Ebay or Craigslist.

3.   They don't make it anymore – Well if you haven't used it in six months, you probably know why it's no longer being made.

4.   It's associated with something sentimental – It may be associated with something sentimental but how important is the sentimental value of an item you haven't thought of in months, or probably years? You only have room in your life for so many mementos.

The test

Here is one way to apply the six-month clutter rule. If you think you've found an exceptional item; one you need to keep even though you haven't used it in months, ask yourself a few questions e.g.

- Can you think of three uses for it?
- If it's a single-use type item, can you think of something you want to do with it in the shortest span of time?
- Why have you not used it in the past six months, if it's so useful?

If you do decide to keep an item, set up a means test. If it works, great! If it doesn't impress you, then you need to go ahead, get rid of that item and start looking for a better option. After considering all these factors, the next phase is determining where to start.

Where to start

It is best to start with cleaning out your closet. You will definitely find items you no longer wear or things that do not fit anymore. Stay away from photographs as the first entry point into Swedish Death Cleaning. Do not start with photographs or personal papers; start out with the large items before tackling the smaller ones. In death cleaning, size matters. Photographs are physical memories; you should probably look into that when your space is cleaned out. With your closet, it is less emotionally taxing to get through. Begin there and perhaps you will be motivated to tackle other parts of your house.

What to Hold on to

You may have kept certain items around the house as a reminder of an experience but you don't need to have the object to trigger a memory. Your mind still holds onto the trip or special day you had that led you to keep a souvenir. Take a look in your kitchen cabinets and make a note of how many plates and glasses you keep. Chances are, you don't need them all.

Discussing death is regarded as a bad omen in some cultures but putting this art of Swedish death cleaning into consideration creates a subtle platform to discuss the topic. A very sensitive aspect of death cleaning is figuring out what items you have that would be useful to your family when you are gone or what properties they'd be keen on keeping. If telling the difference between post-death blessings and burdens becomes a challenge, you can ask your family what they would like to keep from your belongings and discard the ones that wouldn't mean much.

If certain things will be appreciated after you die and you are proud to leave them behind, then keep them but if it will cause any form of distress or ruin the memory of you, then holding on to it would be a lousy idea. For example, if you have embarrassing items in your possession like letters or mails from an illicit affair or fraudulent business deals, getting rid of them should be your main priority.

Things to Document

An important part of Swedish Death Cleaning is involving others. Tell your loved ones and friends what you are up to. This is helpful for a couple of reasons. One reason is, it will help keep you accountable if you tell others of your plan. It also becomes a good time to share with your family your wishes after you pass.

It is during this process that you begin putting together a document that holds any login and password information for any financial institutions or other relevant information that's going to be tough to find after your death.

This concept of Swedish death cleaning is directed specifically at getting people aged fifty and above to start the process of shedding possessions, but this practice doesn't have to be for only people who are way older. The idea can work for all ages; death cleaning should be incorporated to everyone's general lifestyle. Living a life free from clutter and lots of junk you don't need is absolutely therapeutic. The approach is helpful for anyone who wants to simplify and organize their life and not just for people over fifty years of age.

What do you do with all the stuff you are getting rid of? There are many ways to fix that. One way is Gifting. You could sort out your things and thoughtfully gift it to people. Do not offer things that might not fit the recipients taste or space. Carefully think and decide on who receives your gift and would treasure it as much as you did. Another way is to donate to charity or sell the rest off.

Chapter Three

Family or Junk

Overtime, people get attached to their possessions, stuff like couches, pillows, bowls, curtains, paintings etc. We tend to hoard properties by keeping old ones because of certain sentiments or reservations while getting more and more stuff. It could be hard to give out your favorite sweater gotten from a different country or some shoes you were gifted with that you haven't worn in a year.

The Weight of Things after a Loved One's Death

Death may not be a pleasant topic to discuss but it is inevitable and every one of us has to prepare for that. When a loved one passes away, they leave this world sometimes without a final goodbye hug or a goodbye speech. The family is burdened with grief and left to sift through and put away the persons belonging; this is never an easy task.

They are left with unanswered questions, which clothes to keep? Which work files to discard? and What to do with the no longer needed church hats, shoes, bedside alarm clock etc.?

Marie Kondo, author of *The Life-Changing Magic of Tidying Up* advises people to hold on to only those items that provide joy and get rid of the rest with a parting "thank you". But for a while, every item left behind by the departed stirs a raw mix of bittersweet memories and anguished longing. Nothing feels dispensable. Sometimes you try to get along with the day, only to come across an unwanted reminder that the demised person is still gone. At some point, you will begin to wonder if keeping all those objects around is serving a good purpose or prolonging the stage of grief.

This process of cleaning out the effects of a departed loved one sometimes feels like damnation. You're damned if you do, damned if you don't, and like everything else about grief, there are no rules. Considering these grave effects of clutter on a family, what better way to ease the bereavement of your family by simply getting the process done yourself.

Vida Ghaffari is an award winning actress and voiceover artist. She has appeared in quite a number of TV shows and independent films, including 2012's *Cross My Heart*, and has also made a name for herself as a television entertainment reporter.

Until recently, the camera-friendly celebrity was hiding a lot of things behind the scenes. Her Southern California home was packed full of tchotchkes (these are decorative objects rather than functional), as well as clothes, accessories and shoes that she rarely wore.

Ghaffari developed the habits of a collector as a child, when her mother showered her with gifts of Barbie dolls, and later, designer handbags, and insisted they shouldn't be taken out of the boxes. "Look but don't touch" became a way of life for her. She carried over this habit into her adulthood and this led to a home full of clutter, which took both a personal and professional toll. Ghaffari always felt tired and overwhelmed, frequently showing up late to meetings and auditions because she couldn't find the right outfit or makeup.

Her closets were so packed with unworn clothes that she couldn't see what she owned or decide on a shirt without struggle. One day in late 2010, as she was trying to put together an outfit for an important meeting, some extra garments she had placed on the top shelf fell and dropped on her.

This was a liberating moment of clarity for her and she made a resolution to streamline her belongings. She eventually made it a daily practice to see what she could get rid of, later donating 20 bags of stuff to Goodwill. She also gave away lots of clothing and shoes to friends.

As her home became less cluttered and more organized, both friends and colleagues began to note a corresponding transformation in her. She began to feel stronger and more confident. Before long she started getting bookings for more work: She was cast in a supporting role in the much-buzzed-about pilot for *The Mindy Project*, with a star of *The Office*, Mindy Kaling, which aired in September 2012. Producers and casting directors commented that she seemed to be more serious about her work. Even though she wasn't expecting all these benefits from her decluttering, she was pleased with the psychological payoff.

If you look at household clutter from a "feng shui" perspective, Ghaffari's story makes perfect sense. Feng shui also known as Chinese geomancy is a pseudoscience originating from China which claims to use energy forces to harmonize individuals with their surrounding environment. Tisha Morris, the author of the book *Feng Shui Your Life: The Quick Guide to Decluttering Your Home and Renewing Your Life* (Turner, 2011), asserts that our homes mirror our emotional state. Clutter is just stagnant energy; when there is clutter in your home, there will be clutter in you either physically, mentally or emotionally.

Professional organizers, who are hired to help with everything from decluttering closets to restructuring entire homes, routinely see their clients reap emotional rewards. A professional organizer, Hazel Thornton, owner of Organized for Life, a consulting service in Albuquerque, N.M. once stated "It's hard for me to even imagine talking about clutter without talking about the emotional benefits of decluttering, everyone who calls me is either stressed out, frustrated, or feeling inadequate and incompetent in their job, sometimes even guilty.

It is all about emotions; it's even more about emotions than it is about the stuff."

From a different perspective about the subject in question, a significant challenge for most widows is the overwhelming thought of going through a deceased loved one's belongings and trying to decide what do with the items. This is, by far one of the most difficult aspects of widowhood.

Cleaning out the closets does not involve only the bedroom; it includes the home office, the work office, the garage, the basement and the pile of papers that have accumulated since the loss. For many, it is so overwhelming that it is easier to just leave everything as is, for others it is the sad realization that your spouse is not returning and their belongings are clutter you have to deal with. While many may choose to leave the possessions alone for years, others feel a sense of accomplishment organizing the items. It is a personal decision of what works best for the person. Many friends and family members have their opinions of what is right or wrong when it comes to "cleaning out your closets" but the decision solely lies in the heart of the bereaved.

For some people, an immediate reaction to the loss, especially if it was a sudden death, is to quickly clean out everything. The thought process behind this approach is that they will feel better but the real truth is as time goes by, feelings of regret about cleaning out or giving away the items so quickly start to creep in.

As the realization of the loss slowly becomes accepted, they begin to crave some sort of closure by keeping the belongings. After a while, the big question "when do I start to clean and organize my spouse's personal belongings?" starts to pop up.

In many cases, the way clutter affects us has little to do with quantity. A piece of art painted by an ex-lover hanging over the bed can carry more emotional weight than a messy closet full of extra sheets and towels. A chaotic corner of art supplies can feel like an inspiring springboard and a year later, if the supplies haven't been touched, it begins to look like a landscape of failure.

In other words, identifying an item as clutter has more to do with how it feels than how it looks. If you feel less than great in certain rooms or even your entire house, it might be time to target a few items for removal.

There are several types of clutter and here you'll find a guide to the most common kinds, the emotional signals they may be broadcasting, and the effects they could cause in a person's life.

1. Other People's Stuff

Whether its belongings stored for a friend in a garage or basement, or the stuff your kids left behind when they moved out, storing other people's things can be a signal that you need to be more assertive about your space. When other people's properties in your care start becoming a problem, the only solution is setting appropriate boundaries. The home is a template for our own energy. If you decide to let people leave their belongings with you, be very specific about how long you're willing to turn your home into a storage locker.

The belongings of deceased loved ones also fall into this category. After the initial shock of losing someone, it may not feel right to dispose of all their possession. But hanging on to an entire collection of china or unfitting clothes you can't use doesn't honor a loved one's memory. It is advisable to choose a few special items to keep as mementos.

2. Out of the Past

It is good to have a sense of history in a home but making it a temple of nostalgia is not a great idea. You may be holding on to stacks of high school yearbooks or jeans from college that no longer fit which is almost common with everyone but releasing unhelpful reminders of the past can free you up to move forward. When all your available space is filled with clutter, there is no room for anything new to come into your life, your thoughts tend to dwell in the past, and you feel weighed down with problems that have dogged you for some time. You tend to look back rather than forward in your life, blaming the past for your current situation rather than taking responsibility for creating a better tomorrow.

DeAnna Radaj, a home designer based in Charlotte, N.C., encourages clients to let go of items that look nice but are holding them back emotionally. She had a friend who owned a beautiful cashmere sweater given to her by her ex-husband. Every time she'd get a compliment on it and someone would ask where she got it.

These questions would raise uncomfortable emotions to the surface and make her relive everything negative about the relationship. She didn't want to part with the sweater because it was beautiful and expensive. But the cost of an item is not enough reason to keep something that causes you discomfort or distress.

Releasing gifts you are emotionally attached to can take soul-searching work, tears and sometimes even flames. If it requires you to set flames and burn an object that causes you pain, then do that with proper precautions. The process of ditching nostalgic stuff can be profoundly challenging but you can be compassionate with yourself.

When you are dealing with something that is psychologically painful, don't judge or get mad at yourself about it. You don't have to burn down the house you shared with your ex to get rid of the bad memories but you can repaint it, get new sheets for the bed. Simply remodel the space.

3. Unused Goods

Pantries often contain stacks of unused appliances and unused utensils. Home offices are often stocked with boxes of file folders, paper clips and reams of paper that have no hope of ever getting used. Garages also contain a good number of shiny untouched tools, newspapers and sometimes outdoor utensils. Piles of unused stuff can signal a "just in case" thinking which indicates a lack of trust in the future.

It is not bad to keep some extra cookware or tools in case of unforeseen occurrences but when you go overboard, it becomes a problem. If you have lots of clutter you are hanging on to because you think this way, you are sending out a frequency of not trusting, and you will always feel vulnerable and insecure about the future. This can create a bigger cycle of distrust.

Unused items can also represent an unmet aspiration; you might have a juice maker because you plan to learn juice making or a sewing machine that you have not used in a while because you've been busy. There is nothing wrong with having aspirations but your house shouldn't be just a container for your properties.

Figure out if your possessions orient you towards having lots of stuff or being a happy person. The home should be a breather from the world. A place where you can enjoy your family, friends, religion or whatever you're into. Giving away unused belongings, especially those in good condition not only benefits others but can also help you rewrite the story of who you are. Being comfortable with a little empty space helps make room for new things, experiences and even friendships.

4. Incomplete Projects

Having projects in progress around the house is common and, in some cases, quite necessary. Unfinished projects are often accompanied by a sense of failure a lot of times. When half-knitted sweaters or stalled kitchen remodels sit too long, they start to broadcast troubling messages. It is important to acknowledge when you're not finishing a project in a reasonable amount of time.

If something sits untouched for six months with no major life events distracting you then it's time for a review. If you realize you're really not going to finish something, you could donate it. Many charities are eager to pick up unused paint and scrap wood from aborted building projects, and Etsy.com is full of crafters happy to take half-finished quilts and other sewing projects off your hands. Getting rid of those material will be helpful because the subconscious mind knows those unfinished projects are sitting in a drawer or a closet and it's a constant reminder of the presence of an unfinished task.

Try creating a list of all your unfinished projects since some projects need to be completed before others can start, prioritize them. Go through the list and see what is worth your time. If the outcome would be worth the energy you put into it, give it a deadline and make it happen. If you don't finish in that time, give it away and let it go, guilt free. Once you've cleared out looming unfinished projects, you can focus on the ones you care about most in the present. The rewards of that will be ongoing, as will the rewards of getting rid of any other stuff that weighs you down. The freedom that comes with a clear space is tinged with possibility for new experiences.

Chapter Four

A Few Thoughts on Accumulation

A passion for collecting is a healthy outlet and an activity that keeps people connected to the world around them but it can become a baleful enterprise when it crosses the line to hoarding. Hoarding and collecting involve assigning special value to possessions, often values that go beyond the physical characteristics of the object.

For collectors, new possessions become part of a larger set of items and considerable time and energy go into organizing and displaying them. Collecting is healthy when the display or storage of these things does not impede the use of active areas of the home but if a collector expands and loses the ability to keep these new possessions organized, it becomes a hoarding problem. When collecting becomes hoarding, possessions become unorganized piles of clutter that begin to occupy a lot of space. Motivation to display items is lost and the person becomes fearful of others seeing or touching their belonging. This drive increases and causes the person to add more to the collection by acquiring things that would only end up in the pile. Often times once the objects get to the pile, they are seldom looked at again.

There is a misconception about the difference between hoarding and collecting. It is the idea that collectors save valuable things and hoarders save things of little or no value. Although people with hoarding problems often save things others may consider as trash, they also save useful things in excess. Many of them have homes filled with recently purchased items that have never been opened.

Personality differences and Decluttering

De-cluttering and feeling the urge to clean out can be part of a person's personality. There are people that have more organized lives because they want to feel in control and they develop habits like immediately washing the dishes after dinner or wanting everything to be perfectly put in place to give them that sense of power and control. Some other people just don't see the mess or view it as a problem. It is important to recognize these different personality types.

A home that is too cluttered is like an unhealthy body. Keeping the house tidy essentially says something about how ordered, disciplined and well your home is. In reality the models of the homes we see in adverts and consumer magazines with a perfectionist, minimalist aesthetic can be almost unlivable. It is good that people aspire to that but it could be really hard to do in practice because daily life messes it up.

It is advisable for people with personalities that aren't bothered by clutter or how a space looks to note that they will definitely reap the same benefits from organizing as people who are innately more motivated to do it. While one person may not be able to maintain a plan if they feel the rules are too rigid, someone else may need strict rules to abide by in order to stick with the program.

This organizing and cleaning exercise is achievable if you look at what your overall goals are and then decide which steps you want to take. Accumulating junk or hoarding a bunch of stuff you don't need would only become a big problem in the long run. You can become determined to push yourself a little harder than you might be used to by deciding the clear out some of the junk and learn to live with less. While you might think the way you are living now is best for you, you cannot know for sure unless you try something different.

How Tidying Space Affects Mental Clarity

Hoarding is often conceptualized as an anxiety disorder similar to obsessive compulsive disorder. People displace their anxiety onto possessions, surrounding themselves with stuff that allows them to avoid the discomfort of needing to make choices and throw things away.

Thinking about a mess weighs so heavily on a person. It gets worse and worse over time. The size of the mess may stay the same, but the feelings about the mess will get bigger and bigger. Clutter doesn't need to get extremely unbearable before you understand how much the smallest amount of disorderliness can weigh on you. There could be a ton of different, nonserious reasons why your bedroom closet may look like a ransacked outlet of a mall after Black Friday. For many people, it's a time management issue. When the difference is picking up your kids from school on time versus a clean kitchen, the odds are children become the priority but that doesn't mean you should totally ignore that overflowing closet which could be taking a toll on your mental health.

Studies show that living in a disarrayed home space creates a sense of overload, ambiguity, confusion, and over-stimulation in one's everyday life. If clutter and house projects are stressful to you, then streamlining your surroundings may be restorative and relaxing.

In Science, your physical space plays a role in how you behave. For example, surgeons and accountants work better in low-ceiling rooms which promote concentration, while creative types are more productive in bright, naturally-lit rooms with high ceilings. This is just one layer to how our surroundings affect us. The next is a bit more complicated. Every single item in the home carries a story with it and each of these items are constantly whispering to you. For example, a library of books may be telling you to 'Read me, read me, read me.

Everything that is attached to a memory is an invitation to the past. Trips down memory lane can be fun, but living in the past can also be stifling. Because most of these items look backwards in time, they are directly connected to how we perceive ourselves and the story we tell ourselves and carry with us everywhere we go.

It is important to be mindful of where we have been, but all too important to gain clarity of we are headed to. There is a direct correlation between the way we think and the cleanliness of our space. Organizing stuff will save you time because you'll know where to find items when you need them and it also gives you peace of mind. These are all the many ways adjusting space can affect mental health, the overall immune system and the way a person feels about themselves.

Chapter Five

Organizing your Space

Decluttering your home plays an important role in reducing stress and encouraging productivity. From the bedroom to the kitchen, embracing minimalism and letting go of objects you don't need or want can give your home an altogether fresher, more coordinated look as well as help you focus, boost your mood and encourage a better night's sleep. Here are some easy steps to follow in order to organize your home into a stress-free space.

1. Plan Ahead & Prioritize

Organizing your entire home can be a daunting task. To manage it easily, start by planning ahead and prioritizing areas; list all the rooms or areas that need attention and put them in order according to which ones cause the most stress. Another option is to prioritize the workload depending on where you or your family spends most of your time. For example, if you work from home, a good place to start would be your home office or desk space. If you have young children, perhaps their playroom or bedroom would need firsthand attention.

2. Make Some Free Time

Once you have organized each room according to priority, you will need to clear a space in your schedule and dedicate a few hours, a day or even a whole weekend depending on the task. Scheduling this time in your calendar like a regular appointment will help you to avoid distraction to keep putting it off and make the whole process less stressful as you try to fit it in around daily demands.

3. Sweep, Throw Out & Recycle

Before you make your way through your decluttering priority list, take a large box and do a quick sweep throughout your home. Anything you see on a side, table or shelf that you don't use or love, place in the box and move on. Once you've made your way through the whole house you'll be surprised at the amount of clutter you had lying around that had no use or emotional value. After the quick sweep, focus on your high priority areas. Whether you start in the living room, bedroom or bathroom, the same rule applies with decluttering; place all of your possessions into one of three piles: 'Keep' 'Maybe' and 'Throw/Recycle'. The 'Keep' pile should contain items that you use regularly, hold an emotional value or items that you genuinely love.

The 'Maybe' pile is for items that you may not need or want, but you'd like to hold onto a little longer. Everything else that doesn't fall into the 'Keep' or 'Maybe' pile can be thrown away if broken, or recycled/donated.

4. Reorganize

Once you have sorted your possessions, the next step is reorganizing each room into a calming, stress-free space. The key to achieving this is to designate a spot for everything. If you follow the third step correctly, you should have reduced the amount of stuff you have in your home and will have extra room to find a spot for everything you own. Find a space for items that usually sit on surfaces such as keys, books, magazines, letters and phone chargers, and develop a habit of putting them back in their designated place after each use.

Keeping surfaces clear from clutter is one of the simplest ways to encourage a peaceful mind as you aren't constantly distracted by mess.

Another method of organizing is the SPACE approach where SPACE stands for; Sort, Purge, Assign, Containerize, and Equalize.

Sort: Sort your things by category rather than focus on cleaning one location, such as a room, dresser or closet at a time. The root of the problem lies in the fact that people often store the same type of item in more than one place. You can sort your properties in the following order of categories;

- Tops (shirts, sweaters, etc.)
- Bottoms (pants, skirts, etc.),
- Clothes that should be hung (jackets, coats, suits, etc.)
- Socks, underwear
- Bags (handbags, messenger bags, etc.)
- Accessories (scarves, belts, hats, etc.)
- Clothes for specific events (swimsuits, uniforms, etc.), shoes,

- Books, papers (credit card statements, greeting cards, instruction manuals, etc.) photos and miscellaneous items.

Resist the urge to return items that you think belong in another room straight away; put them in a dedicated box and return them at the end of the process to avoid always being distracted.

Purge: Get rid of items in each category that are broken, useless, superseded or otherwise irrelevant. If you haven't used an item in a long while, ditch it. This is an area where your own personal judgment becomes important. If you fail to purge anything during a cleanup, you'll probably find it harder to keep everything organized.

Assign: With purged and sorted groups of items, you can assign each group a permanent home that doesn't necessarily need to be in the room where you have done the sorting, again making use of your own preferences and existing habits, and bearing in mind any space restrictions. Ideally, this should involve saying "this item goes in this furniture/ library area", rather than just in a particular room.

Containerize: Minimizing clutter means having somewhere to put stuff away and that is where storage containers (for example new bookshelves or racks) become important. However, it is better to hold off on stocking up on bins, containers, and other storage items until you determine what you have first. More bins do not equal more organization. It just adds to the clutter. Having dedicated locations for everything also makes it easier to put everything away.

Equalize: The final key to staying clutter-free is dedicating time every day (or every week for less frequently used rooms) to equalize: return everything to its home. This is basically maintaining the order you have already put in place.

The Benefits of decluttering your space

Throughout this book, we have discussed the importance of practicing Swedish death cleaning as a lifestyle. Anyone with an overflowing closet or totally stuffed basement can attest to the stress caused as a result of the piles of junk. That's because not only is it annoying to look at, but it can dredge up so many different emotions. Clutter comes with a lot of baggage, both literally and figuratively. When I look at my messy closet, I definitely feel some type of way. I feel stressed at the lack of organization, and I feel confused as to what kind of style I'm going after or what outfit to even pick out. Clutter can have quite the psychological effect.

In a study published in the *Journal of Applied Developmental Psychology* and notes, it states that "This line of research studies the effects on children of living in what is termed as a chaotic environment. The focus is not the interpersonal chaos that may preside in some homes; that too has dire effects. Rather, the focus is on physical settings that are noisy and disorganized. Children who live in these settings have more than their share of problems. There is a connection between junk and other problems. We can all feel it when our desks are messy, or our kitchens out of sorts. It's unsettling, and can hold you back from getting stuff done in other areas of your life.

Getting rid of clutter is quite the chore, but it can have profound effects on other areas of your life. Here are some proven benefits of finally clearing out clutter.

1. It helps you let go of the past - The psychological impact of certain objects in your possession can be hard to ignore. Keeping a bunch of mementos that you do not necessarily need makes it hard when it's time to move on. There are certain things we struggle to part with because of sentiments but know deep down we can't keep stashing away. Clearing out your space gives room for new projects, new ideas and even new relationships.

2. It aids concentration - Too many things in your surroundings can have a negative impact on your ability to

focus and process information. Neuroscientists at Princeton University found this when they analyzed the task performance of a set of people in an organized versus disorganized environment. The results of the study showed that physical clutter in your surroundings competes for your attention, resulting in decreased performance and increased stress. Clutter essentially makes your brain multitask, so getting rid of it enhances productive concentration.

3.   It boosts creativity – Many artsy types love the idea of a messy desk or studio but working in a minimalist environment actually helps the creative process.

Dividing your attention between several stimuli like a messy desk, twitter feed or a novel's plot hole often results in increased stress and decreased creativity/productivity. This also depends on the person, what kind of project in progress, and how much concentration is needed.

4. It improves the quality of sleep - Do you ever lie in bed and stare, with utmost discomfort, at your messy closet or the piles of laundry on the floor? The average adult needs about 7-8 hours of sound sleep. It's amazing that anyone could get any rest in a disarrayed room because there is a connection between messy rooms and a lack of sleep. A new sleep study has found that people who doze in cluttered rooms are at a high risk for developing

hoarding disorder and are more likely to have sleeping problems. This includes having trouble falling asleep at night and experiencing rest disturbances. An uncluttered bedroom enhances rest and brings about better sleep.

5. It boosts a person's mood - Clutter can make you feel cranky not only because it's like visual noise, but it also sends a signal that you don't have your life together. This connection was shown by researchers at UCLA's Center on Everyday Lives and Families (CELF), who studied the relationship between thirty-two California families and the thousands of objects in their homes. Clutter has a profound effect on our mood and self-esteem. It can make one feel overwhelmed, stressed and even

sick. Coming home to a neat and tidy space actually lifts your spirit and keeps you in a good mood.

6. It enhances focus - When you let junk pile up, it all stands as a reminder of the things you haven't accomplished. This can be good at first, for example a yoga mat in the corner can remind you to finally start stretching in the morning but eventually that yoga mat turns into clutter when it remains unused for months at a time. You might get around to reading that huge stack of old motivational books one day, or lose some pounds and fit into those unworn pants hanging in your closet. But the reality is that we hang onto far more objects than we need, and, instead of motivating us, they become talismans of guilt and shame.

A study that analyzed how different women described their home environments found that those who considered their spaces more cluttered, unfinished, and less restful had consistently higher levels of the stress hormone cortisol and worse moods over the course of a day compared to the other women who described their homes as being more restorative.

Other research has found that clutter can actually make it harder for the brain to focus on a specific task basically because the visual cortex gets distracted by the irrelevant information you take in. Keep things that inspire or motivate you, but get rid of anything that makes you distracted and feeling out of place.

7. It is one way to become happier - "Swedish death cleaning" fits into the minimalism movement. Psychologically, minimalism is based on the idea that happiness doesn't come from stuff, but rather from relationships and experiences. When you get rid of the excess stuff surrounding you, you can better identify those things that are really important and bring pleasure and joy in your life. Studies have actually shown people who are more focused on materialistic pursuits like getting rich and buying stuff are at higher risk of becoming unhappy, anxious, having low self-esteem and even developing problems with intimacy.

8. It relieves stress.

When you start living in a clean, organized space, you will find that you become less stressed and also more focused. Having fewer things to worry about really can make life seem more manageable, from practical chores carried out on a day-to-day basis to big projects and problems you face. Multiple studies link clutter with stress and decreased productivity. When there is less chaos on the outside, we're likely to feel less chaos on the inside.

9. It helps keep the mind active.

As the aging process can be sometimes distressing with the accompanying isolation and boredom, death cleaning could serve as a means to keep the mind active and at the same time serve its sole purpose. It also gives the 'cleaner' a good reason to visit friends and family thereby helping to foster relationships which become very important as we age.

Letting go of clutter can be difficult, but the benefits far outweigh any negatives. Learn to let go of excess junk, and reap the benefits of a more minimalist life.

Making it Last

Exploring a new approach to something is not always easy. It takes an average of thirty- one days to form a new habit. When embarking on any new project, it is imperative to note that consistency and discipline are essential to getting outstanding results. As the saying goes, Discipline is the bridge between goals and accomplishments. The practice of Swedish Death Cleaning requires constant effort, commitment and discipline especially when dealing with personal possessions. Consistency is key if you want to make any habit stick. Living life daily with less clutter and sentimental baggage is attainable if you are willing to make it a habit. It is easy to make it last when you start simple, stay consistent and also get a partner or someone who would support you through the process. You could create a to-do list or mark dates on your calendar when you take out time to go through stuff you might have accumulated in a little while and do a clutter check.

Understanding Swedish death cleaning would go a long way in helping families to discuss sensitive issues that might otherwise be hard to bring up. It is a nice, proactive approach to facilitating cooperation and communication among families early on in the aging process. There is also something very empowering and healthy about taking care of your own space and making it more organized while you're still around. It is advisable to start thinking about death cleaning as soon as you're old enough to start thinking about your own mortality. Learn not to collect things you don't want.

Death cleaning has amazing benefits for older people, their families and anyone who understands the essence of the concept. People engage in a type of death cleaning without calling it that when they downsize from a large house to a small apartment as they get older, for instance.

It's a new way of thinking about the grunt work that comes along with those transitions, which can be really stressful. It cannot be overemphasized that a cluttered home reduces productivity and creates tension in the environment. As adults get older, having a house full of stuff may also raise their risk for falls and create other health and safety hazards.

Death cleaning is an ongoing process that's never truly finished. No one knows the day they will leave this world so death cleaning is a continuous process.

After a gruesome task of decluttering, it is alright to reward yourself but reward yourself in a new way as well. Go see a movie or grab a cupcake, don't go shopping to buy a bunch of new stuff that will only turn to more clutter at the end of the day. Also, teach yourself to appreciate things without actually buying them. It might take a while to get used to but training yourself to admire things by merely looking instead of buying them is a good practice.

One last thing to note is a personal question; will anyone be happier if I save this? This is a good way to frame the inner monologue debate that will go on in your mind as you declutter. A bunch of cards or letters you treasured from middle school probably isn't going to mean anything to anyone other than you.

Conclusion

Life is a totality of our choices and experiences, short but beautiful. It is therefore very important that we take some time to look back and see how far we have come. This is the point where Döstädning as a lifestyle practice plays a supportive role.

This art of death cleaning enables people to focus on only the tangible experiences and memories they have gathered over the years. Humans naturally have a tendency to go overboard when accumulating stuff over the years but continually letting go of things that aren't necessary useful anymore by decluttering keeps your home tidy and improves the overall quality of life.

There is a charity aspect of Döstädning which involves donating some of your properties to people who are less privileged in your society. This charitable act will go a long way in helping those in need, promoting generosity in your family, and also give you a feeling of accomplishment. It brings a sense of satisfaction to a person, inducing civic engagement and is said to improve happiness.

Life itself is about humanity, you do not need a million bucks before you can make a difference. Donating old books to a school library or giving out that warm wool sweater you don't wear anymore to someone who needs one will make all the difference.

Taking charge of your environment by decluttering and intentionally making efforts to put the emotional wellbeing of your loved ones first is a healthy and beneficial lifestyle. The train of Swedish death cleaning is one which everyone should get on and encourage others to do so too as it is a simple way of making the most out of experiences, saving only what is relevant and promoting mental health.

Made in the USA
Monee, IL
04 December 2019

17928840R00046